The Library of Sexual Health™

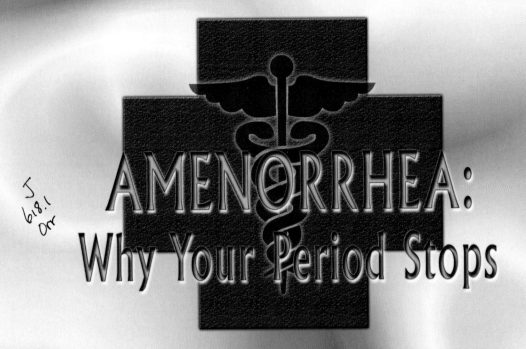

AMENORRHEA:
Why Your Period Stops

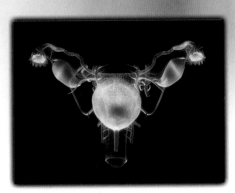

TAMRA B. ORR

ROSEN
PUBLISHING®

New York

To my Dad, the first person to make me feel like I could do anything I wanted—and never stopped believing

Published in 2009 by The Rosen Publishing Group, Inc.
29 East 21st Street, New York, NY 10010

First Edition

Library of Congress Cataloging-in-Publication Data

Orr, Tamra B.
Amenorrhea: why your period stops / Tamra B. Orr.—1st ed.
   p. cm.—(the library of sexual health)
Includes bibliographical references and index.
ISBN-13: 978-1-4358-5061-3 (library binding)
1. Amenorrhea. I. Title.
RG171.O77 2009
618.1'72—dc22

                      2008016736

Manufactured in Malaysia

CONTENTS

INTRODUCTION

"On the rag." "The monthlies." "Aunt Flo is visiting." "Code Red." "The curse." It goes by a lot of names including "that time of the month," but it all refers to the same thing—your period. It is a normal part of your life from adolescence until usually your mid-fifties. For almost all women, it keeps coming back month after month for decades. For some, however, the situation is different. Either the woman's period doesn't start when it is supposed to, or it starts but then disappears. Under certain circumstances, this condition is called amenorrhea.

In order to understand what can go wrong with your period, you need to understand how the female reproductive system works. With most of your reproductive system located inside your pelvis, it can be hard to learn exactly what it is doing and why. Most of the time, all the different parts function together smoothly, thanks to a combination of very complicated natural processes. When something goes wrong, however, it can have a domino effect that results in a condition in which your period stops—or never starts in the first place.

Take a look at the illustration on page 6 of the female reproductive organs. At the very top, you see the two fallopian tubes, one on either side of your pelvis. Each hollow fallopian tube averages four to five inches long and is only about as big around as a single strand of spaghetti. The open ends of the fallopian tubes flare out near the ovaries. These are oblong, almond-sized organs that are amazing egg holders. When you are born, they contain more than one million immature, pencil point–sized eggs. You will never produce more of these eggs; the ones you have when you are born are it. The purpose of these eggs is to be fertilized by a male's sperm to create an embryo and, eventually, a baby. Ovaries not only hold your eggs; they also secrete (produce and release) two extremely important female hormones, or chemicals, called estrogen and progesterone.

After you begin menstruating, one of the eggs inside your ovaries matures every month and is released into the nearby fallopian tube. One month the egg may come from

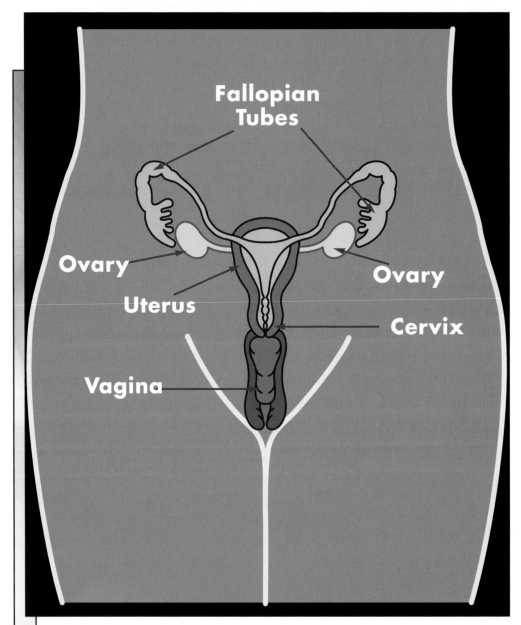

The female reproductive organs are located within the pelvis, in the lower abdomen. Each of the organs shown here is crucial to good sexual health.

the left side, while the next month it may come from the right. As tiny as that egg is, it takes several days for it to complete the long journey through the tube all the way to the uterus.

The uterus has one main purpose: to nurture a developing fetus, or unborn baby. After you ovulate (release an egg), thanks to the production of hormones, blood flows to the lining of the uterus, causing the uterus to thicken. This occurs so that if the egg is fertilized by a sperm and becomes an embryo, the uterus is ready to accept and nourish it. If a woman is not sexually active, then the blood in the lining of the uterus is not needed. The unfertilized egg will pass out each month along with the unnecessary uterine lining, creating a woman's monthly period. This sounds rather simple, but it isn't. The process depends on certain hormones being produced just at the right time and in just the right amounts.

Most females take their periods for granted. It is a part of life that women do not enjoy but accept as necessary, since it will allow them to have children someday. However, approximately 2 to 5 percent of women cannot take the process for granted, as they have amenorrhea. How and why it happens is what this book is all about.

CHAPTER ONE

Understanding Your Monthly Cycle

A lthough there are a lot of jokes made about it, puberty is really an amazing thing. It takes a child and begins the process of turning that child into a man or a woman. Puberty happens quite differently in males and females, of course. In males, almost everything is on the outside, where they can see the changes taking place. In females, on the other hand, many of the changes of puberty take place on the inside.

For girls, puberty usually begins between the ages of eleven and fourteen. The national average in the United States is 12.8 years old. During puberty, your body goes through some tremendous changes. When you were younger, you and young boys looked a lot alike. You were both straight as sticks with flat chests and no hips to speak of. When puberty hits, however, all of that changes.

First, you begin to get taller. Since you typically hit puberty before boys do, that means for a year or so, you will probably be taller than most of the boys. Don't worry—they will catch up with you later when their growth spurts kick in.

Next, your hips and thighs will begin to widen, giving you more of a curve in your figure instead of being straight up and down. This widening will one day help you carry a baby. For right now, it means clothing fits a lot differently than it used to.

One of the most noticeable changes occurs when your breasts begin growing. First, your nipples will begin to stick out farther, and a breast will appear as fat deposits develop around your milk glands. How big your breasts will be, what shape they will take, if both sides develop at the same pace—all of that is unknown. Unfortunately, in our society, the size of a girl's breasts has taken on more importance than it needs to. The truth is, breasts come in all shapes and sizes, and whatever yours happen to look like is just the way they should be.

As you turn from a young kid into a young woman, you will notice hair growing out of places it has not grown from before. Pubic hair will begin to grow under your arms. It will also grow between your legs and in a triangle over your pubic bone. This hair is often a different or darker color than what you have on your head. It is also curly, even if your hair is straight. In addition, the hair on your arms and legs will tend to get darker during puberty, and you will begin to sweat more often. Your oil glands will increase production, which may make your hair look

As you go through puberty, it is natural to explore your body's changes. Getting used to having breasts and how they affect your appearance may take some time.

greasy faster and your face break out in pimples or acne. You will probably find that you need to shower more often and use deodorant.

THANKS TO HORMONES

Along with all of your outward changes, internally you are getting ready to start your period. That is the official mark that says your body is maturing and you are now physically able to become a mother. For the average girl, periods begin between the ages of eleven and fourteen, although it can be as early as nine and as late as sixteen. At first, these periods are pretty irregular. You may have one, then another one in a few weeks, and then nothing for several months. All of that is completely normal. Your body is still trying to get things figured out, and it can take up to a year or more before your body settles into any real pattern. Once your periods do settle into a pattern, they will tend to be between two and eight days long, and they will occur every twenty-six to thirty-two days.

What is happening inside to cause you to begin your period? The short answer is that your hormones are becoming more active. Hormones are chemicals in the body that are produced by certain organs, glands, or special cells. Hormones circulate throughout your body in the bloodstream. They have to stay in balance and be released at just the right times and in just the right amounts for many different body processes to go smoothly.

In females, there are four main hormones that work together to cause puberty and then help maintain a woman's menstrual cycle. The first one is estrogen. It is responsible for the development and maintenance of the lining of the uterus, the control of fluid within the body, and the preparation of the ovary for the release of the egg.

The second hormone is progesterone. It is responsible for preparing the lining of the uterus to accept and nurture an egg. Progesterone also plays a role in getting the breasts ready to fill with milk for breastfeeding and for making sure the fetus grows strong and healthy, should pregnancy occur.

Follicle stimulating hormone, or FSH, is the one responsible for helping the eggs in the ovaries to mature, while the luteinizing hormone, or LH, triggers ovulation to start and helps the other hormones to do their jobs. When it comes to the reproductive system and puberty, the proper functioning of these four hormones is crucial.

SUPPLIES ON HAND

When you first start having periods, it can be confusing trying to figure out what to do. A trip to the store can only make it more confusing, as you are hit with a huge variety of choices. There are pads (or sanitary napkins, as they are sometimes called). They come in overnight, light days, extra long, deodorized, extra absorbent, and maxi varieties. Pads are placed inside your underwear and act like sponges. The bottoms of these pads are sticky so that they will stay in place. Some of them even have sticky "wings" that wrap around the crotch of your underwear to keep them from shifting as you go about your day.

Tampons are another choice. These are also like sponges, but they are inserted inside the vagina rather than worn outside. Some come with either a cardboard or plastic applicator that makes it easier to slide the tampon in. Some do not have these, and you simply use your fingers to do the job. Tampons have strings attached to

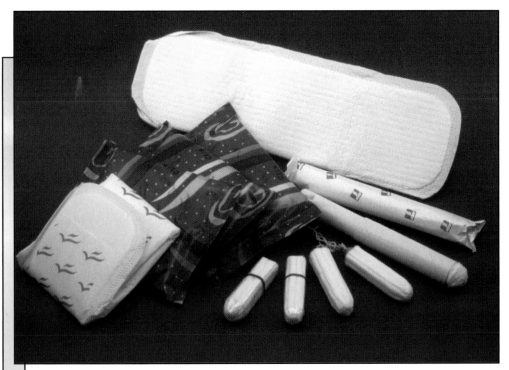

Figuring out which kind of product to use during your period is often a trial-and-error process. Each girl is unique. Experiment with different kinds of pads and tampons to see what works best for you.

Making a Chart

Charting your menstrual cycle is easy. By observing the patterns of your periods, you can discover what is normal and natural for you.

Keeping a chart of your periods will help you understand your cycle. You can get a good idea of how regular you are—or aren't. You can better plan for when your next period is going to start and make sure you have the supplies in your medicine cabinet, purse, or backpack. You will also have a helpful history to show a physician.

On the chart, put an X on the first day of your period. Continue to make X's until the day your period stops. On the days with the heaviest flow, you might want to color the box in. On days with serious cramps, you can put a C. You can also save a place on the chart for making notes about each period, such as "It was exceptionally heavy" or "Very light flow."

If you don't want to keep an official chart like the one described here, at least note the days your period starts and stops. (You can write it down in your journal or diary or on a calendar.) This way, you'll have the basic data to know your cycle's pattern. And if you do have to see your doctor, you will be able to tell him or her some crucial information. Looking back at your record is one of the best ways to learn if you have a problem.

them so that when the tampon is saturated with blood, you can pull it out.

Both pads and tampons are made from highly absorbent cotton, and they both will soak up the blood from your period. There are advantages and disadvantages to each product. For example, tampons are easier to carry in your purse than pads. They are smaller and do not take up as much room. Tampons are invisible from the outside, so no one can tell you are having a period. In addition, they are usually the neater option, since your underwear will tend to stay cleaner than with pads. You can wear a tampon when you go swimming, but you cannot wear a pad, as it will soak up water. On the other hand, pads are easier to use, especially for a girl who is not yet comfortable with the idea of putting something into her vagina. Most girls will end up using a combination of pads and tampons, depending on the day, the flow, and the situation. Take time to experiment with each one and see what suits you best.

COPING WITH CRAMPS AND OTHER SYMPTOMS

Monthly periods may bring along some physical symptoms that can be unpleasant. Your breasts may feel tender and swollen right before your period starts. You may also have cramps, or uterine spasms that cause lower-back and pelvic discomfort. For some girls, these cramps are so mild that they are hardly noticeable. In others, they can be severe enough to send a girl to bed for a day or two. Most girls fall somewhere in the middle of those extremes.

Cramps often vary from month to month. One cycle, you may not even notice them; the next cycle, they may interfere with your daily activities.

Coping with cramps depends on how severe they are. For the majority of women, applying heat through a heating pad, hot bath, or hot-water bottle and/or taking specially formulated over-the-counter medications are enough to make cramps manageable. If that isn't enough, however, and cramps are literally sending you to bed in pain each month, talk to your parents about it. They can help you make an appointment with a gynecologist—a doctor specializing in treating the female reproductive system. Occasionally, there are underlying medical problems that cause painful periods, and you should make sure that these are not the cause of the discomfort.

Along with these pain symptoms, periods may also cause your body to retain (hold on to) extra water. This can make you feel puffy and bloated, or make your favorite jeans fit tighter than usual. After your period starts, you will shed this extra water and lose the feeling of being bloated.

All of these symptoms together create a condition that is known as premenstrual syndrome, or PMS. PMS often includes "roller-coaster" emotions. You may feel more irritable or sensitive, you may find that you are snapping at your friends and family or crying more easily than usual. This is all due to the shifting hormones in your body. While you cannot help how you are feeling, you can control how you demonstrate it. Getting enough sleep and taking extra good care of yourself will help you keep your emotions under control. If you do feel like the rest of the world is treating you unfairly, remember that it is the hormones talking and not you.

These issues surrounding ovulation and periods can vary greatly, depending on the person. Some girls have not yet started their periods, and, therefore, these issues are not yet part of their lives. For others, their periods are more or less regular and come with predictable symptoms. Still others may have very irregular periods that start at odd times or perhaps have stopped altogether. Occasionally, irregular periods are due to health issues—structural abnormalities or hormonal imbalances, for instance. When health issues cause the cessation or absence of monthly periods, the girl is suffering from amenorrhea.

Amenorrhea is not a disease or health problem in and of itself. Instead, it is a symptom of another condition. The following chapter will discuss who is affected by amenorrhea and why it occurs, as well as what can be done to change it.

CHAPTER TWO

Will It Ever Get Here? Primary Amenorrhea

Y ou have watched your friends go through it month after month. Their periods start. They get the stuff they need. They complain about cramps. They get used to their periods. Throughout that time, you just watch and wonder when is it ever going to happen to you. It's not that you especially want to have periods—you can tell they are a hassle. Yet, you feel left out or even worried.

DELAYED MENARCHE

The majority of the time, the later onset of periods is not true primary amenorrhea. It is more likely due to delayed puberty, also called delayed menarche. This simply means that you start puberty later than others. Your friends probably got breasts before you did, they got acne before you did, and now they have gotten their periods before you. You may have a slightly slower internal time clock than they do, and there is nothing wrong with you at all. It may have to do with your body build as well. If you are exceptionally thin or athletic, you are likely to start your period later than others.

It is possible, however, that the delay in puberty is primary amenorrhea. Doctors define primary amenorrhea as not having any signs of puberty by the age of fourteen (no breast development or pubic hair) or not having menstruation start by the age of sixteen. Primary amenorrhea occurs in less than 1 percent of the females in the entire United States, so it is not a common condition.

THE HYPOTHALAMUS-PITUITARY AXIS

There are several possible reasons for primary amenorrhea. The most common reason is that the ovaries are not functioning properly. There may be several different causes for this condition. For instance, ovarian failure may be due to a hormone imbalance originating in the hypothalamus, a gland found at the base of your brain. The hypothalamus is the control center for several important processes in your body. Although tiny, it controls your body temperature, your blood pressure, and your appetite. The hypothalamus also directly controls the pituitary gland, which, in turn, controls the endocrine organs throughout the body. The following conditions may cause your hypothalamus and/or pituitary to function improperly, leading to primary amenorrhea:

- **Extreme exercise.** For many young girls, the hypothalamus does not function properly because of

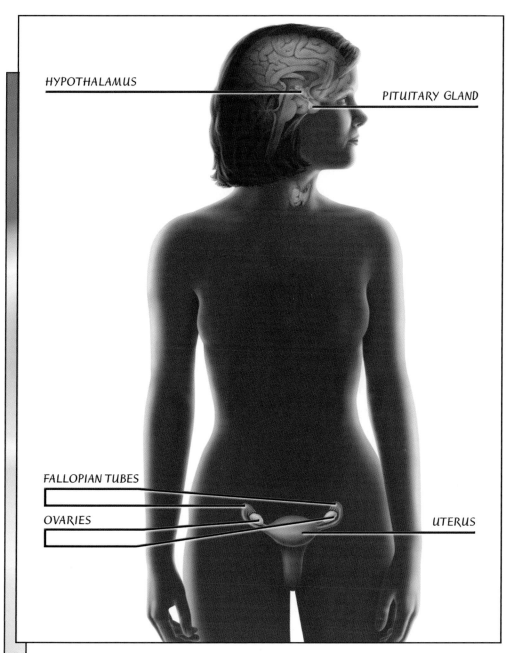

HYPOTHALAMUS

PITUITARY GLAND

FALLOPIAN TUBES

OVARIES

UTERUS

The hypothalamus and pituitary gland are located in the brain. They communicate with the reproductive organs by releasing hormones that circulate in the bloodstream.

things they are doing to their bodies. For example, an extreme exercise regimen (more than eight hours of intensive exercise each week) can disrupt the function of the hypothalamus. Studies show that menarche is delayed later and later as young girls increase strenuous athletic training.

- **Malnutrition.** Your hypothalamus will not function properly if your body is not getting proper nutrition and hydration. For this reason, the eating disorder anorexia nervosa can be especially dangerous for girls who have not yet started their periods. Anorexia nervosa most commonly affects teen girls, in whom it often causes secondary amenorrhea. However, anorexia is also a known cause of primary amenorrhea in preteens who have not yet begun their periods. Without the right balance of nutrients in the body, the ovaries cannot function properly. If they don't release their hormones, your period never starts. Over the long term, anorexia nervosa and other forms of malnutrition can also cause infertility, bone loss, and stunted body growth.

- **Pituitary gland.** Primary amenorrhea may occur because of a tumor or abnormal growth on the pituitary gland. This is a small gland in the middle of your brain that is itself controlled by the hypothalamus. Often referred to as the "master gland," the pituitary gland releases hormones that affect growth and the development of the reproductive system. In males, the pituitary gland tells the testes to release testosterone. In females, it stimulates the release of several hormones, including luteinizing hormone (LH) and follicle stimulating hormone (FSH), discussed in chapter 1. LH and FSH are both needed to create and release mature eggs from the ovaries. Once LH and FSH are released, the hormones estrogen and progesterone are also released. This sends a signal to the uterus to start filling up its lining with nutrient-rich blood in case a fertilized egg arrives.

- **Psychological stress.** Being under a lot of mental or emotional pressure can actually create a hormone imbalance that delays the onset of your period.
- **Other behaviors and conditions.** Other behaviors and conditions that negatively affect the hypothalamus include long-term disease, chronic drug use, and sudden weight gain or loss.

PINPOINTING THE CAUSE: GENES AND CHROMOSOMES

In some cases, ovarian failure (another form of primary amenorrhea) is not directly related to the hypothalamus or pituitary. Instead, it is caused by underlying chromosomal abnormalities, or problems with your genetic makeup. These are most likely congenital, or already in place when you were born. Some chromosomal abnormalities result in a lack of adequate eggs and follicles needed for regular ovulation and menstruation. Periods may start and be sporadic, or they may not start at all. Girls with Turner syndrome, for instance, have only one X chromosome instead of the usual two. As a result, their ovaries contain "streaks" of nonfunctional tissue and cannot produce adequate amounts of hormones to start menstruation. By taking estrogen pills, many girls with Turner syndrome can eventually begin having their periods, but fertility will remain a challenge for them.

Other uncommon causes of primary amenorrhea are genetic conditions in which a girl's reproductive organs do not develop properly during fetal development (growth inside the womb). Girls with Mayer-Rokitansky syndrome have complete reproductive systems, but a structural abnormality in the uterus and/or vagina prevents menstrual blood from flowing out normally. Surgery can often repair this problem.

Primary amenorrhea is relatively rare, and diagnosis of and treatment for it can be extensive. This type of amenorrhea is easy to diagnose—there are no periods. However it can be very challenging for physicians to figure out what exactly is causing the problem in the first place. It takes patience, tests, and time. It helps to know that primary amenorrhea does not necessarily mean that you will have problems with sexual health or fertility in the future.

Ten Great Questions to Ask Your Doctor

1. What is causing my periods to be so late?

2. How long does it take for a cycle to become regular?

3. How much exercise is considered too much?

4. What is a normal body weight for a female of my age and body type?

5. How might amenorrhea affect my decision to become sexually active in the future?

6. How might amenorrhea affect my future ability to bear children?

7. If I have amenorrhea, does it mean I could pass it on to my future daughters?

8. How do I handle the discomfort of cramps?

9. What would happen if I started taking birth control pills?

10. Can amenorrhea be a lifelong experience, and if so, how will it affect me?

CHAPTER THREE

Where Did It Go?
Secondary Amenorrhea

Y ou have had your period for some time now. You have been keeping track of your cycle, and, although it does seem to be a bit irregular, it is slowly beginning to establish a pattern. Then you notice that you have not had one for a while. You can't remember exactly when the last one was. After looking in your journal or on your chart, you realize that you have not had a period in a couple of months. Actually, it has been even longer than that. What is going on? Is there a problem? Should you be worried?

If you have had periods previously, even only a few, and then they stop for six or more months, this is considered secondary amenorrhea. (Of course, this is assuming you are not pregnant, which naturally puts an end to your period.) Secondary amenorrhea is more common than the primary form, affecting between 2 and 5 percent of the women in the United States.

Along with missing your periods, other symptoms may come along with secondary amenorrhea. Each one

It may sound wonderful to have your periods go away for a while. In reality, however, a lack of periods can signal a problem that needs to be checked out by your doctor.

is due to an imbalance of the hormones. A milky white discharge from your nipples may occur because of an extra release of progesterone. Excessive hair growth on your face or torso is possible due to an overproduction of a male-related hormone called androgen. Vaginal dryness sometimes occurs due to a lack of enough estrogen, and headaches and vision changes may also occur due to elevated levels of prolactin, a pituitary hormone.

Who is most at risk for secondary amenorrhea? Experts say those who have less than 17 percent body fat, who suffer from anorexia nervosa, who are obese, and/or who take hormone supplements run the highest risk of secondary amenorrhea. As with primary amenorrhea, this condition can also be caused or made worse by physical and psychological stress.

Pointing Out a Cause

If you are an adolescent female, the most common immediate cause of secondary amenorrhea is low body weight (80 percent or less of what is considered normal). Estrogen release is based, in part, on the amount of fat cells in your body. If you lose a lot of weight and body fat, the amount of estrogen you produce will drop dramatically as well. So, if you go on a crash diet, your periods may slow down or completely disappear.

Anorexia nervosa, a serious eating disorder, is also a common cause of low body weight and, therefore, amenorrhea. In fact, the absence of a girl's period is one of the criteria used to diagnose anorexia nervosa. Periods may cease prior to significant weight loss, meaning that amenorrhea can be seen as an early warning sign that something is wrong. Anorexia is very dangerous and can be difficult to treat.

Anorexia nervosa affects mostly female teens, causing them to severely restrict the amount of food they eat in order to control their weight. The resulting lack of iron, zinc, and healthy dietary fats interferes with hormone function and leads to the cessation of periods. Bulimia, a disorder in which affected people eat a lot (binge) and then force themselves to vomit (purge), also results in poor nutrition and may cause amenorrhea.

Secondary amenorrhea can also be caused by low body weight associated with overexercising. This is especially the case for young women involved in sports that demand a lot of energy, such as ballet, gymnastics, and long-distance running. As your body weight drops, so do your estrogen levels, potentially causing your periods to stop. In addition, low estrogen levels affect how much calcium you take into your bones. If it is not enough, you can have weak bones and develop a serious condition like osteoporosis. Combine weak bones with high sports demands and you are much more likely to end up with shin splints, bone spurs, and fractures.

There are several reasons why your periods stop, some of which do not apply to adolescent females—

Hard-core training regimens can reduce overall body fat to less-than-ideal amounts. For many female athletes, this causes secondary amenorrhea.

menopause, for instance. Some of these other causes of secondary amenorrhea are:

- **Pregnancy.** If you are not sexually active, then pregnancy is not a possibility. When a fertilized egg embeds in the uterine lining, the female reproductive system responds by stopping further ovulation and, hence, menstruation.

- **Menopause.** This is a phase a woman goes through, usually in her fifties, when she is no longer fertile and her cycle stops for good. Clearly, you are far too young for this to happen.

- **Surgery.** A woman may no longer get her period if she has had her ovaries removed or if she has had a hysterectomy, an operation in which the uterus is removed. This is rarely done to young, healthy women, but it is done as treatment for older women who have serious health problems such as large fibroid tumors, severe endometriosis, or endometrial or cervical cancer.

- **Illness and medication.** Having a long, serious illness can stop your menstrual cycle. Certain medications will also do it, but your doctor or pharmacist probably will have already told you about this possible side effect. If you have been using contraceptives like the Pill or injected hormones and you stop, this, too, can disrupt your cycle. It takes an average of three to six months for your cycle to resume, although some women return to normal periods more quickly.

- **Hormonal imbalance.** Having too much of one hormone and not enough of another can prevent ovulation. Women who have polycystic ovary syndrome (PCOS) have an imbalance of estrogen and testosterone that interferes with their cycles. A pituitary tumor can also cause the condition. The tumor often causes

Lactational Amenorrhea

One other normal time when women may lose their periods for a while is after they have babies and are breastfeeding. The sucking action of the nursing baby suppresses the production of hormones that are needed for ovulation. It works best under specific conditions. For example, the baby must be primarily breastfed, and the baby should be nursed on demand, rather than on a set schedule. Doing this can result in a new mother not having any periods for anywhere from a few months to more than a year. For many new mothers, this is a relief and a side effect of mothering that they truly appreciate!

problems with the production of various hormones, upsetting the delicate balance of how and when they are released.

- **Thyroid problems.** Hypothyroidism can cause secondary amenorrhea. Here, your thyroid gland is not working hard enough, creating a low thyroid hormone level and affecting your cycle.
- **Damage from surgery.** A condition known as Asherman's syndrome occurs when scar tissue has built up on the lining of the uterus due to surgical procedures like a Caesarean-section (C-section) or a D and C (dilation and curettage).

Secondary amenorrhea is a symptom that is more common than primary amenorrhea but is not necessarily any easier to diagnose. Often, doctors have to do thorough tests that look at many different systems within your body to figure out just what is going on. If a woman is neither pregnant, pre-menopausal, nor nursing, then solving the mystery of where her periods went is a complex one. Like primary amenorrhea, secondary amenorrhea does not necessarily mean you will have future sexual health and fertility problems. Much depends on the cause of the problem. Often, the underlying health issue causing the secondary amenorrhea can be solved through medication, surgery, or other treatments.

Myths and Facts

MYTH: If I haven't started my periods by the age of fourteen, then something is wrong with me.
FACT: Although many girls have started by fourteen, it is not uncommon for menstruation to begin at age fifteen or sixteen, particularly if other women in your family have started their periods later.

MYTH: If I don't have periods, then I can't get pregnant.
FACT: Just because you are not having periods does not necessarily mean that you are not ovulating. You can still get pregnant, and with such an irregular cycle, you may not even realize that you are pregnant.

MYTH: If my periods don't start, then I will never have breasts or hips.
FACT: Breast and hip development begins even before your cycle starts. Most likely, you will have these changes around the age of fourteen, whether or not your period has started by that time.

MYTH: If I don't have periods, then I am one of the luckiest girls in the world.
FACT: While periods can be a hassle, they are a part of your development and will one day play a part in your becoming a mother. If you are sixteen or older and don't have any periods, then you should see a doctor.

CHAPTER FOUR

What Will the Doctor Say—and Do?

Say you have reached the age of sixteen and your periods have not started yet, or you have been having a regular cycle and now your periods have stopped for months. In either case, it is time to see your pediatrician/family doctor or possibly a gynecologist to find out just what might be going on inside of you. Amenorrhea is not a threatening problem in and of itself. However it may be a signal of a more complex and risky condition that needs to be identified as soon as possible.

GETTING A MEDICAL HISTORY

When you go to the doctor, he or she will most likely ask you a set of questions, including:

- What was the date of your last period, if any?
- Are you sexually active?
- Do you use any kind of birth control?
- Has your weight changed dramatically recently, either a gain or loss?

- What is your monthly menstrual pattern, if any?
- Was your flow heavy or light?
- How far apart were your periods?
- How much physical and emotional stress are you currently under?
- What kind of exercise do you get? How often do you exercise? How long?
- Are you taking any prescription medicines?
- Are you taking dietary supplements?
- How is your acne?
- Have you noticed hair growing excessively on parts of your body that do not normally grow hair?
- Have you had any secretions (fluids) issue from your nipples?

Your answers to these questions will provide the information your doctor needs to begin to know what might be wrong.

TIME FOR AN EXAMINATION

Typically, your detailed medical history will be followed by examinations and tests. First, you will get a typical physical exam that may include any or all of the following:

- Measurement of height
- Measurement of weight
- Measurement of body mass index

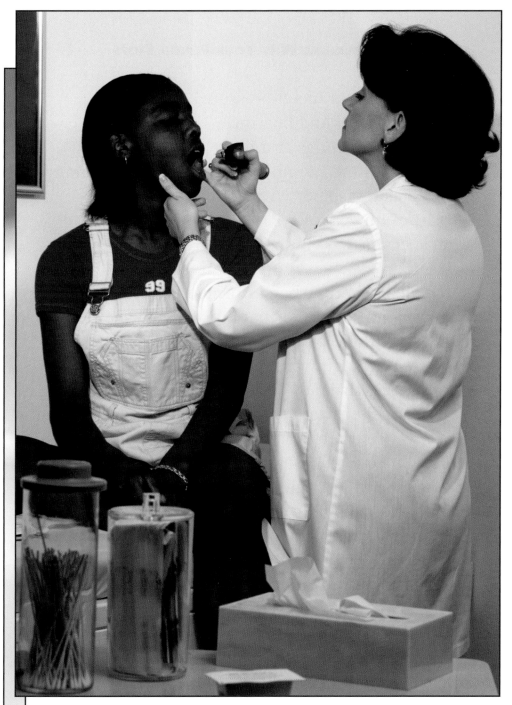

Seeing your doctor about menstrual problems often involves the same kind of examinations you have had in the past for school, sports, or camp.

- Measurement of blood pressure
- Check of vision and hearing
- Listen to your lungs and heart
- Palpate/feel the lymph nodes and thyroid gland, as well as the spleen, liver, and kidneys
- Breast exam
- Pelvic exam

A pelvic exam may be performed for females who are having problems with their periods. If you have never had a pelvic exam, then it can be a somewhat unnerving experience. You might want to take along your mother, sister, aunt, or girlfriend. Being with someone who has undergone a pelvic exam can be comforting.

For a pelvic exam, you will lie back on the doctor's table, usually covered in a paper or cotton gown from the waist down. Your feet will be placed in metal foot holders called stirrups, which are attached to the examining table. They will help support your legs throughout the examination.

In this position, your knees will fall over to either side. This allows your doctor to be able to see between your legs. Being exposed like this makes many girls and women feel quite vulnerable. Remember that the doctor is a professional who only wants to help you. Take deep breaths and relax as much as you can, as that will make everything easier for you.

WHAT WILL THE DOCTOR SAY—AND DO?

First, your doctor will examine the external part of your genitals, looking for swelling, sore spots, or anything else that does not appear as it should. Next, your doctor will do a bimanual exam. This means that he or she will carefully place one or two fingers of one hand into your vagina and then, using the other hand, press on the outside of your lower abdomen and pelvis. This

Physicians use various special medical tools to help them in their examinations. For instance, an OB/GYN may use a vaginal speculum *(above)* to get a better view of a female patient's internal reproductive organs.

way, the doctor can feel your uterus, fallopian tubes, and ovaries. He or she is searching for any tenderness or swelling. While you will feel some pressure, this part of the examination should not cause you any pain. Then, the doctor will take a plastic or metal tool called a speculum and insert it into your vagina to open it up and make it wider. This way, he or she can see the vaginal walls and your cervix. Once again, the doctor is checking for any infection, growths, or other abnormalities. If you are curious about what you look like, most doctors are quite willing to hand you a small mirror and let you look inside.

If you are sexually active or if you have a family history of cervical cancer, then your doctor may also take a Pap smear. A Pap smear is a swab of your cervical cells, which will be put on a slide and examined under a microscope in a lab. An irregular Pap smear can be a sign of cancer, infection, or other problems.

Usually, this is the end of the internal exam. The speculum will be removed so that you can put your legs together and sit back up. While it sounds like a lot of things to do, this exam typically lasts about ten to fifteen minutes total.

Time for Tests

Your doctor may order a battery of different tests, depending on your medical history and the results of your examinations. Some of the most common ones include:

- Pregnancy tests
- Blood tests to check for levels of various hormones
- Urine tests for hormone levels
- Thyroid and adrenal function tests

The progesterone challenge test is another common test for a woman who is having trouble with her menstrual cycle. For this test, the doctor gives you the hormone progesterone for seven to ten days, usually as a pill, and watches to see if it causes uterine bleeding. If you do bleed, it indicates that you probably have anovulation, or you are not releasing a mature egg mid-cycle, as is normal. However, if you do not bleed with the progesterone challenge, it indicates that you may have a problem with the follicle stimulating hormone (FSH).

Ultrasound, computed tomography (CT), and magnetic resonance imaging (MRI) are other diagnostic tools that can help your doctor find out what is causing your amenorrhea. These are especially useful for showing if you have a tumor or other structural abnormality.

Ultrasound

Ultrasound works by sending out sound waves to create an image of what is under the skin. You cannot feel these waves, so the test itself is pain-free. A vaginal ultrasound is done by inserting a thin, smooth probe into your vagina to take an up-close look at your uterus, cervix, and ovaries. The probe can feel rather cold, but it should not hurt.

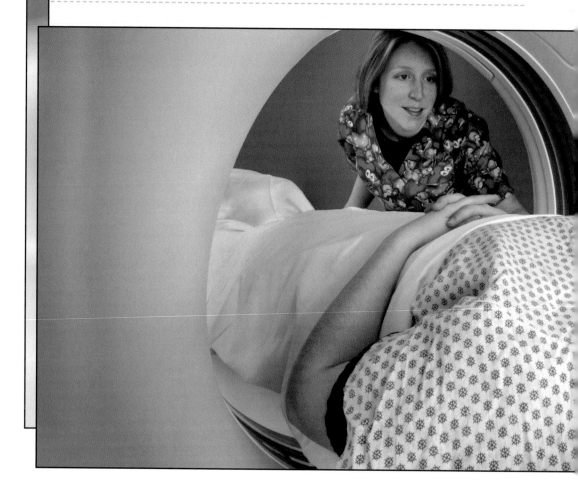

Computed Tomography

Computed tomography is a simple procedure for the
patient. It does not hurt at all, and it is quick. You start off
by lying on a table while a special doughnut-shaped scanner
ring holding a very low radiation X-ray tube moves over
your head. You might be injected with a dye that helps to
make certain tissues (and tumors) easier to see on the
scan. The dye will not hurt you, although some people

A CT scanner *(left)* is a high-tech diagnostic tool that can reveal a lot about what is going on inside of you. Like standard X-rays, CT scans do not cause the patient any discomfort at all.

say it makes them feel warm or gives them a metallic taste in their mouth when it is first injected.

As the tube moves around you, it takes multiple images from different angles. The test may last from thirty to ninety minutes, and while you stay perfectly still, the table may shift now and then. The scanner sometimes makes odd clicking or buzzing noises, but this is normal and harmless.

The X-ray beam is sent directly to an electronic detector, and this information is forwarded to a computer. The computer analyzes the information it receives and then merges it together to cast an image on a television screen. The radiologist will "read" what he or she sees there and create a report for your doctor.

Magnetic Resonance Imaging (MRI)

An MRI is a scan similar to a CT. It works using radio waves and magnets to create an image of what is going on inside your body. The magnets are so powerful that you need to remove your jewelry and other metal objects before entering the scanning area. As with the CT, you start off by putting on a gown and lying on a table. But then you slide inside a long, hollow tube or cylinder. For some people who struggle with being in small, enclosed spaces (claustrophobia), this may feel quite uncomfortable and even scary. If you feel that way, simply tell the radiologist. He or she will know of ways to make the experience easier for you.

As with the CT scan, you may be given a special dye with the MRI. It is given through an intravenous drip and helps the radiologist to see certain types of tissues better. MRIs usually take between thirty and sixty minutes to complete. While you are inside the cylinder, you will hear a variety of odd sounds, from knocks and bangs to the sound of drums. If the noise bothers you, let the people know and they will give you a set of earplugs.

Ten Facts and Statistics

1. Less than 1 percent of adolescent girls in the United States develop primary amenorrhea.

2. Between 2 and 5 percent of women in the United States develop secondary amenorrhea.

3. Puberty tends to start between the ages of eleven and fourteen for girls.

4. The average age for puberty in girls is 12.8 years old.

5. Primary amenorrhea is defined as not starting any signs of puberty (breast development and/or growth of pubic hair) by age fourteen and no periods by age sixteen.

6. Secondary amenorrhea is defined as not having periods for six months or more after cycles have initially started.

7. Treatment of amenorrhea is based on what its original cause is.

8. Amenorrhea is a symptom, not a disease or health condition.

9. Eating disorders are one of the main causes of both primary and secondary amenorrhea.

10. Diagnosing the condition causing amenorrhea is often complicated because there are so many different body systems involved.

CHAPTER FIVE

Taking Care of Yourself

As we have seen, amenorrhea can be the symptom of a number of different conditions, from birth defects to a tumor to eating disorders. While some of these are completely out of your control, there are other factors that you do have some ability to control. For example, you can generally decide how much you exercise, how much and what you eat, and what your stress level is from day to day.

GETTING FIT—AND STAYING HEALTHY

Everyone knows that exercising is good for you. It keeps you fit and healthy and strengthens your bones and muscles. However, too much of a good thing is not good. Exercise-associated amenorrhea occurs when the body is using up so much energy by training that it begins to shut down other functions. This usually happens only to high-level athletes or women who are addicted to exercising. Some of the high-risk sports associated with amenorrhea:

- Cross country
- Track and field
- Swimming
- Cycling
- Rowing
- Diving
- Figure skating
- Gymnastics
- Ballet

If you are involved in a sport, then you should add up how much time you spend training for it. Is it more than eight hours a week? How intense is the time? It's one thing to spend an hour practicing basketball free throws and another thing to do endless laps around the track.

Running is one of the sports that can easily lead to amenorrhea. Long-distance running, especially, requires a great deal of energy and stamina.

They are entirely different levels of intensity. If your lack of periods is associated with too much exercise, then find a way to limit the amount. Talk to your coach. Talk to your parents. Find a way to cut back. You could also look into other types of exercise that require less energy, such as golf, archery, or horseback riding.

EATING WELL

Another way that you can lower your risk of getting amenorrhea is to make sure you are not too thin or falling prey to eating disorders, such as anorexia or bulimia. Between five and ten million young people today suffer from one of these problems. Those with anorexia eat severely restricted diets. Often, these individuals also overexercise. They lose far more weight than is healthy, yet they don't even realize it. When they look in the mirror, they see someone who is still fat and needs to keep losing weight in order to be attractive. It is certainly understandable why some girls get obsessed with their bodies in today's society. Thinness is a high priority, and many consider it the key to being attractive, wealthy, successful, and loved.

GETTING DE-STRESSED

The other factor that can lessen your risk of developing amenorrhea and that remains under your control is the amount of stress you deal with on a regular basis. According to a University of Michigan study, more than two-thirds of teens surveyed reported that they feel stressed out at least once a week, and one-third say they feel completely stressed out on a daily basis. At your age, stress can come from a lot of different directions, including:

- School demands
- Responsibilities at home

Runway models like the one shown above may seem as though they have perfect bodies. In reality, many models are dangerously underweight.

Reaching for the Unobtainable

"Supermodels in all the popular magazines have continued to get thinner and thinner. Modeling agencies have been reported to actively pursue anorexic models. The average woman model weighs up to 25 percent less than the typical woman and maintains a weight at about 15 to 20 percent below what is considered healthy for her age and height. Some models go through plastic surgery, some are 'taped-up' to mold their bodies into more photogenic representations of themselves, and photos are airbrushed before going to print. By far, these body types and images are not the norm and [are] unobtainable to the average individual, and far and wide, the constant force of these images on society makes us believe they should be. We need to remind ourselves and each other constantly (especially children) that these images are fake."

(Excerpt from Something Fishy: Web site on Eating Disorders—www.something-fishy.org)

- Extracurricular activities
- Part-time jobs
- Problems with friends
- Changes in your body
- Family relationship difficulties
- Moving
- Family and/or personal financial problems

What can you do to cope with all of these stressors? First of all, cut out any of the stresses that you can. You might have to talk to your parents, coach, teachers, or friends about it. Maybe they can give you some ideas or suggestions for lightening the load.

Of course, having a health condition like amenorrhea is a stressor as well. Some ways to help manage this stress include:

- Regularly eating healthy meals. (Caffeine and sugar will not help your stress or your health.)
- Learning and using relaxation exercises, such as deep breathing and meditation.
- Getting enough sleep each night—which, at your age, means at least eight to nine hours.
- Taking regular breaks. Before you come home and start your homework, take some time to get a snack, relax a bit, and let go of some of the day's tension.
- Talking to your friends about how you are feeling or writing it down in a daily journal. Sometimes, just sharing what you are feeling is enough to help reduce stress.
- Talking to your school counselor.
- Asking your parents if you can see a therapist or counselor who can talk to you and help you figure out ways to make life less stressful.
- Exercising moderately.

What else can you do if you have amenorrhea? Some physicians will prescribe an oral contraceptive, also known as the Pill, which can help regulate periods. The Pill and other hormonal medications do have some potential negative side effects, however, so there is some risk in

Meditation and other relaxation techniques can reduce your stress levels. This not only helps with physical problems but also improves your emotional state.

using them. Your doctor should carefully discuss with you the risks and benefits of these medications, as well as ask you detailed questions about your own health and family history. Your answers will help determine if hormonal contraceptive medications are right for you.

Hormone replacement therapy involves taking different kinds of supplemental hormones such as progesterone or estrogen, usually in pill form. In some cases, taking these appropriate, doctor-prescribed hormones can help balance a woman's cycle enough to regulate it. Again, do not take these until you have talked it over with your family and consulted with your doctor.

Are there any other types of treatment doctors will recommend for amenorrhea? Some may give you nutritional advice such as taking vitamin and mineral supplements that support the female reproductive system. There are physicians who will also recommend additional, alternative medicine treatment, including massage, acupuncture, and homeopathy.

Most girls consider their periods to be quite a tedious monthly hassle. However, it shifts from boring to worrisome when those periods either don't arrive at all or arrive but then disappear again. Knowing about amenorrhea is important. If you think you have amenorrhea, do the right thing.

Most of the time, amenorrhea is not a serious condition, and once identified, it is very treatable. The first step is communicating with someone you trust and sharing your concerns and questions. Start with your parents and then, perhaps, talk to your family doctor. Yes, periods can be an annoying part of your life, but having regular and routine periods gives you peace of mind. It will also let you join your friends as they joke about that good old "time of the month."

GLOSSARY

adrenal Related to the adrenal glands, part of the endocrine system.

amenorrhea The condition of having no periods by the age of sixteen (primary amenorrhea) or established periods that disappear for at least six months (secondary amenorrhea).

anorexia nervosa Eating disorder characterized by eating too little food and losing too much weight.

cervix Bottom part of the uterus at the top of the vagina.

computed tomography (CT) scan Special X-ray used for imaging internal organs.

embed To lodge or become fixed.

estrogen Hormone that is made in the ovaries and plays a large role in the development of female sex characteristics.

fallopian tubes Four- to five-inch-long tubes that carry the egg from the ovaries to the uterus.

gland Body organ that produces and secretes substances.

gynecologist Doctor that specializes in treating conditions of the female reproductive system.

hypothalamus Gland in the brain that controls your blood pressure, body temperature, appetite, and reproductive systems.

magnetic resonance imaging (MRI) Scan of the internal organs of the body using radio waves and magnets.

menstruation Part of a female's monthly reproductive cycle. Unneeded blood and an unfertilized egg are shed from the uterus.

osteoporosis Medical condition characterized by weak bones due to a lack of calcium.

ovaries Small organs that hold immature and mature eggs in women's reproductive systems.

pituitary gland Gland in the brain that affects growth and reproductive systems.

progesterone Hormone produced by the ovaries that affects a woman's menstrual cycle.

puberty Process of changing from a child into an adult.

speculum Plastic or metal tool inserted into the vagina to facilitate a pelvic exam.

sporadic Occurring at irregular intervals.

suppress To hold back or prevent.

ultrasound Way of taking pictures of internal organs using sound waves.

uterus Also called the womb, the portion of a woman's reproductive system that carries a baby.

vagina Four- to six-inch-long passage that connects to the uterus and leads to the outside of the body.

FOR MORE INFORMATION

American College of Obstetricians and
    Gynecologists (ACOG)
P.O. Box 96920
Washington, DC 20090-6920
Web site: http://www.acog.org
(202) 638-5577
ACOG is a private, voluntary, nonprofit organization of
    professionals providing health care for women.

American Society for Reproductive Medicine (ASRM)
1209 Montgomery Highway
Birmingham, AL 35216-2809
(205) 978-5000
Web site: http://www.asrm.org
ASRM is a professional organization committed to the
    advancement of reproductive medicine. It develops
    educational materials and programs for professionals,
    patients, and other interested parties.

National Institutes of Health (NIH)
9000 Rockville Pike
Bethesda, MD 20892

(301) 496-4000

Web site: http://www.nih.gov

Part of the U.S. Department of Health and Human
Services, the NIH is the primary federal agency for
conducting and supporting medical research, including
studies on children's and teens' health.

National Women's Health Network
514 10th Street NW, Suite 400
Washington, DC 20004
(202) 347-1140
Web site: http://www.womenshealthnetwork.org
The National Women's Health Network works to develop
and promote a health care system that is guided by
social justice and reflects the needs of diverse women.

WEB SITES

Due to the changing nature of Internet links, Rosen
Publishing has developed an online list of Web sites
related to the subject of this book. This site is updated
regularly. Please use this link to access the list:

http://www.rosenlinks.com/lsh/ame

FOR FURTHER READING

Ashby, Dr. Eve Anne. *Puberty Survival Guide for Girls.* Lincoln, NE: iUniverse, Inc., 2005.

Bailey, Jacqui. *Sex, Puberty, and All That Stuff.* London, UK: Franklin Watts, 2005.

Bourgeois, Paulette. *Changes in You and Me: A Book About Puberty Mostly for Girls.* Toronto, ON: Key Porter Books, 2005.

Dickerson, Karle. *On the Spot: Real Girls on Periods, Growing UP, and Finding Your Groove.* Cincinnati, OH: Adams Media, 2005.

Kreitman, Tricia, et al. *The Period Pocketbook: Honest Answers with Advice from Real Girls.* Berkeley, CA: Ulysses Press, 2006.

Morais, Joan. *A Time to Celebrate: A Celebration of a Girl's First Menstrual Period.* Bel Air, CA: Lua Publishing, 2003.

Pascoe, Elaine. *Teen Dreams: The Journey Through Puberty.* Chicago, IL: Blackbirch Press, 2004.

Weschler, Toni. *Cycle Savvy: The Smart Teen's Guide to the Mysteries of Her Body.* New York, NY: HarperCollins, 2006.

BIBLIOGRAPHY

Aetna InteliHealth, Inc. "Health A to Z: Amenorrhea."
Updated March 2, 2007. Retrieved March 12, 2008
(http://www.intelihealth.com/IH/ihtIH/WSIHW000/
9339/9443.html).

Dickerson, Karle. *On the Spot: Real Girls on Periods, Growing
UP, and Finding Your Groove.* Cincinnati, OH: Adams
Media, 2005.

eMedicineHealth's Consumer Health. "Amenorrhea."
Updated October 24, 2005. Retrieved March 19, 2008
(http://www.emedicinehealth.com/amenorrhea/
article_em.htm).

FamilyDoctor.org. "Amenorrhea: What You Should Know."
Updated March 2008. Retrieved March 19, 2008
(http://familydoctor.org/online/famdocen/home/
women/reproductive/menstrual/885.html).

Gravelle, Karen, and Jennifer Gravelle. *The Period Book.*
New York, NY: Walker and Company, 2006.

Mayo Clinic. "Amenorrhea." Updated May 15, 2007.
Retrieved March 19, 2008 (http://www.mayoclinic.
com/health/amenorrhea/DS00581).

MedlinePlus Medical Encyclopedia. "Amenorrhea."
Updated May 10, 2006. Retrieved March 19, 2008

(http://www.nlm.nih.gov/medlineplus/ency/
article/001218.htm).

Merck Manual Online Medical Library. "Amenorrhea."
Updated November 2005. Retrieved March 19, 2008
(http://www.merck.com/mmpe/sec18/ch244/
ch244b.html).

Otis, Carol L. *The Athletic Woman's Survival Guide.*
Champaign, IL: Human Kinetics Publishing, 2000.

Penn State College of Medicine. "A to Z Topics:
Amenorrhea." Retrieved March 19, 2008 (http://
www.hmc.psu.edu/healthinfo/a/amenorrhea.htm).

University of Virginia Health System's Adolescent
Medicine. "Amenorrhea." Updated February 12, 2004.
Retrieved March 19, 2008 (http://www.healthsystem.
virginia.edu/uvahealth/peds_adolescent/amenr.cfm).

WebMD. "Sexual Health: Absence of Periods." Retrieved
March 19, 2008 (http://www.webmd.com/
infertility-and-reproduction/guide/absence-periods).

Weschler, Toni. *Cycle Savvy: The Smart Teen's Guide to
the Mysteries of Her Body*. New York, NY:
HarperCollins, 2006.

INDEX

ABOUT THE AUTHOR

Tamra B. Orr is the author of more than one hundred nonfiction books for people of all ages. She has a degree in English and education, as well as a minor in public health and safety, from Ball State University. She loves reading books as much as she does writing them. Orr is the author of books on other sexual health topics, including teen pregnancy, date rape, and ovarian cysts and tumors, as well as a book on benign tumors. She lives in the Pacific Northwest with her husband and four children.

PHOTO CREDITS

Cover, © www.istockphoto.com/mammamaart; cover, p. 1 3D4Medical.com/Getty Images; 4 (silhouette) © www.istockphoto.com/jamesbenet; p. 6 © www.istockphoto.com/Thomas Paschke; p. 10 © Phanie/Photo Researchers, Inc.; p. 13 © Cordelia Molloy/Photo Researchers, Inc.; p. 14 Shutterstock.com; p. 16 Bay Hippisley/Taxi/Getty Images; p. 21 © Articulate Graphics/Custom Medical Stock Photo; p. 27 © www.istockphoto.com/dndavis; p. 30 Greg Trott/Getty Images; p. 37 David Buffington/Photodisc/Getty Images; p. 39 Keith Brofsky/Stockbyte/Getty Images; pp. 42–43 Lester Lefkowitz/Stone/Getty Images; p. 47 © www.istockphoto.com/Jacom Stephens; p. 49 Karl Prouse/Catwalking/Getty Images; p. 52 © www.istockphoto.com/David Crowther; back cover (top to bottom) 3D4Medical.com/Getty Images, © www.istockphoto.com/Luis Carlos Torres, © www.istockphoto.com/Kiyoshi Takahase Segundo, CDC, © www.istockphoto.com/Amanda Rohde, Scott Bodell/Photodisc/Getty Images.

Designer: Nelson Sá; **Editor:** Christopher Roberts
Photo Researcher: Amy Feinberg